Daniel And The Spanish Robot

Daniel's Toys

Today, just like every day, the Spanish robot said hello in Spanish as soon as he saw that Daniel was awake:

Today the Spanish robot wanted to teach Daniel how to say some toys in Spanish.

So he wrapped some of Daniel's toys so Daniel could guess what the Spanish words meant!

The first thing the Spanish robot brought out was **un balón**.

Daniel carefully felt the shape. He then quickly unwrapped it to find…..

un balón

Un balón was a ball.

Yes! He was right!

The next thing the Spanish robot brought out was **un osito**.

It was soft.   It had two legs and two arms.

Daniel carefully unwrapped the parcel to find….

un osito

Un osito was a teddy!

Yes! he was right again!

The next thing the Spanish robot brought out was **una muñeca**.

It was soft. It had two legs and two arms. He only had one teddy that was like that! Not knowing what it was he unwrapped it to find….

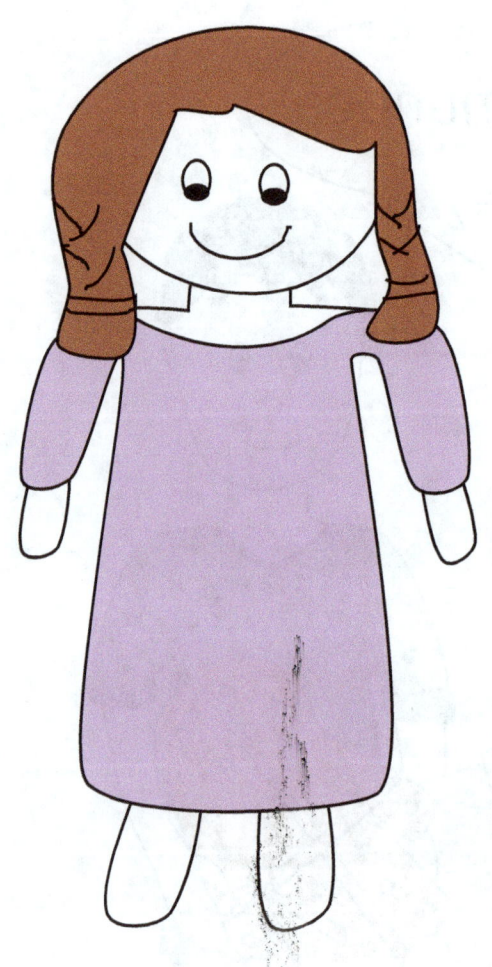

una muñeca

Una muñeca was a doll. A DOLL !!!

"Hey! That's not mine!" thought Daniel. "My cousin must have left that when she was playing here yesterday!"

The next thing the Spanish robot brought out was **un barco**.

un barco

Daniel felt carefully the shape.

Daniel thought he could recognise this toy.

He unwrapped it to find….

Un barco was a boat!

Yes! he was right!

For the last object the robot led Daniel into the back garden:

una bicicleta

This time Daniel didn't need to feel it's shape. He knew exactly what it was! He ripped off the paper quickly to find…

Una bicicleta was a bike!

Yes! he was right again!

It had been a fun day. Can you remember all the Spanish words for the toys? Let's say them together!

un balón

un osito

una muñeca

un barco

una bicicleta

Now Daniel knew how to say his toys in Spanish he could ask the robot for his toys:

The Spanish robot was very pleased that Daniel had remembered the Spanish word for a ball and that **por favor** was the Spanish way of saying please, so he went and got a ball.

They both then played together in the garden until Daniel's cousin called round for the doll she'd left at Daniel's house yesterday. Daniel was now able to tell her that **una muñeca** was the Spanish way of saying a doll.

Daniel And The Spanish Robot

Daniel Helps Papá Noel

It was a cold December morning when the Spanish robot got an urgent message from **Papá Noel**:

Papá Noel needed help! The Spanish robot went quickly to get Daniel. Father Christmas must be *very* busy. So they needed to help **Papá Noel**!

It didn't take long to get to where **Papá Noel** lived as the robot could fly there. When they arrived the robot saw a beautiful Christmas tree so he told Daniel to look at the tree:

¡Mira el arból de Navidad!

Es bonito.

¡Hola!

Daniel said in Spanish that it was pretty. The truth is though he found *every* Christmas tree pretty! **Papá Noel** looked happy to see them. He greeted them with a friendly "**Hola**".

Papá Noel wanted to check he could remember all the Spanish words for some toys. Let's say them with Papá Noel:

- un osito
- una muñeca
- un balón
- un barco
- una bicicleta

The Spanish robot was very impressed that **Papá Noel** had remembered correctly the Spanish words for the lovely toys.

The first thing they were asked to do was to count how many scarves there were:

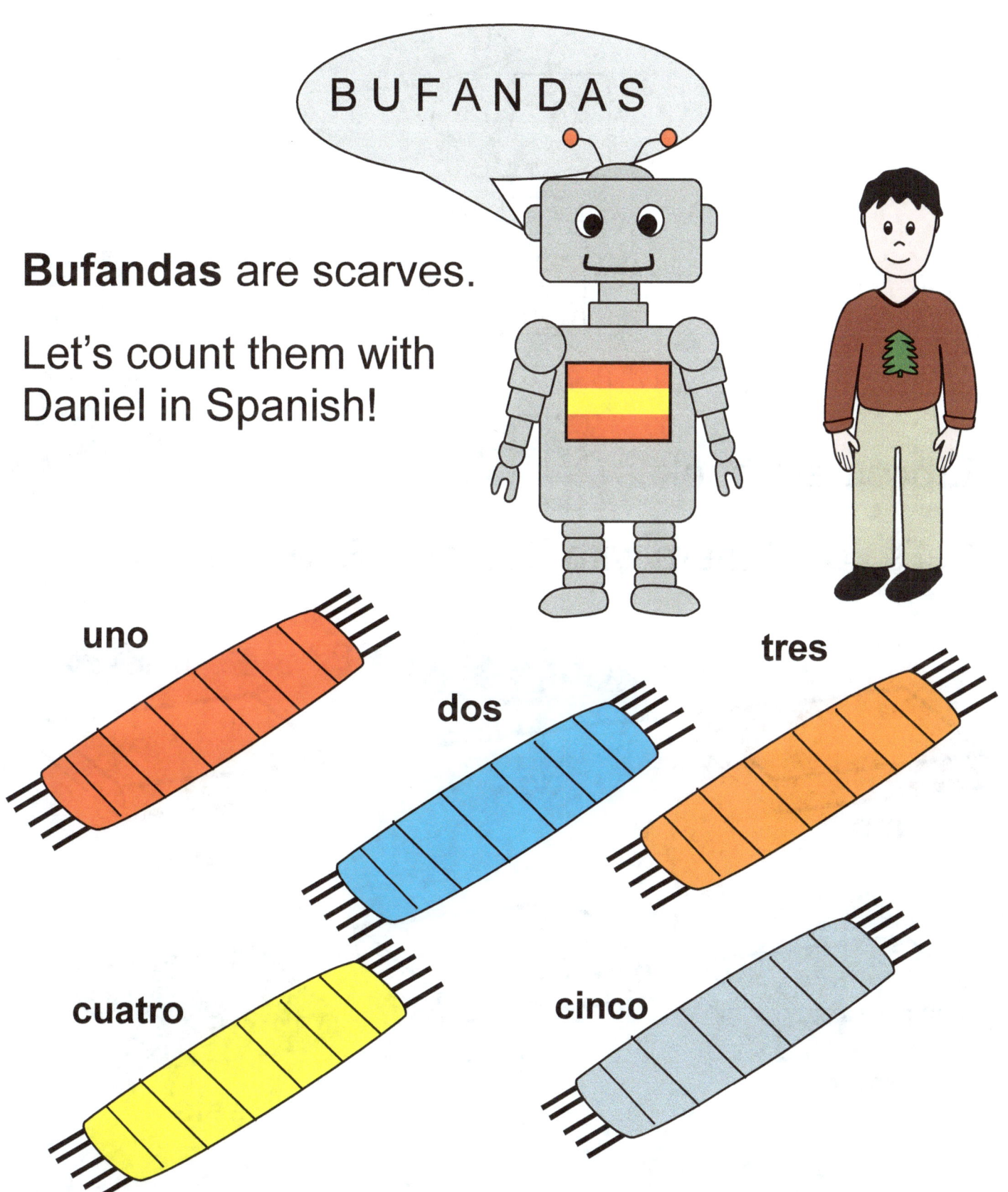

BUFANDAS

Bufandas are scarves.

Let's count them with Daniel in Spanish!

uno

dos

tres

cuatro

cinco

Hay cinco bufandas.   There are five scarves.

Next they counted how many books there were:

Libros are books.

Let's count them with Daniel in Spanish!

Hay seis libros. There are six books.

Daniel quickly picked up the paper which was the colour **rojo**. He was very happy he remembered that **rojo** was red. Daniel and the Spanish robot then wrapped lots of presents:

1　2　3　4　5　6　7　8　9　10
uno　dos　tres　cuatro　cinco　seis　siete　ocho　nueve　diez

Hay diez regalos. (There are ten presents.)

Papá Noel was so happy that Daniel and the Spanish robot had helped him that he asked Daniel what he'd like to take home with him today.

Now Daniel had seen lots of amazing toys but he *didn't* ask for any of these things!

Instead he said:

Un libro, por favor.

Papá Noel went away and returned with……

un libro

Papá Noel brought Daniel a book all about trains.

Daniel told everyone that the book was for his dad.

Es para mi padre.

Papá Noel thought it was so lovely that Daniel had chosen something for his dad instead of himself, that he also let him choose something for his mum:

Una bufanda para mi madre, por favor.

Papá Noel went away and returned with……

una bufanda

Daniel was so happy that he now had all his Christmas presents. He had:

 **un libro** for his dad

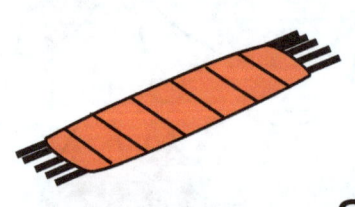 **una bufanda** for his mum

and

 **un balón** for the Spanish robot

The ball for the Spanish robot was just a spare ball Daniel had, but he thought the robot would like it.

It had been a fun day and Daniel wanted to stay more but he had to be home for dinner, so they all waved goodbye and said " **Adiós**."

Spanish - English word list

Hola	Hello	Gracias	Thank you
Adiós	Good bye	Mira	Look
Por favor	Please	Ayúdame	Help me!

Numbers

1	2	3	4	5	6	7	8	9	10
uno	dos	tres	cuatro	cinco	seis	siete	ocho	nueve	diez
one	two	three	four	five	six	seven	eight	nine	ten

Toys

 un balón — a ball

 un barco — a boat

 un osito — a teddy bear

una muñeca — a doll

 una bicicleta — a bike

Christmas presents

 un libro — a book

 una bufanda — a scarf

Family

 mi padre — my dad

 mi madre — my mum

Christmas words

 Papá Noel — Father Christmas

 un árbol — a tree

 el árbol de Navidad — the Christmas tree

 regalos — presents

Let's sing a song!

The following words could either be sung to a made up tune, or you could try saying the words as a rap.

For inspiration of a melody to use you could hum first a nursery rhyme. How many different versions can you create using the lyrics?

 un balón, un balón

 un osito, un osito

 una muñeca, una muñeca

 un barco, un barco

 una bicicleta, una bicicleta

 un libro, un libro

 una bufanda, una bufanda

 un árbol, un árbol

Follow on activity:
Take 4 pieces of paper. Write one of the below words on each piece, and do a picture.

| un osito | un balón | un barco | una muñeca |

Can you remember the order the toys appear in the story "Daniel's Toys"? Arrange the words in the correct order. Look at the story or the song lyrics to see if you are right!

© Joanne Leyland   First edition 2017 2018   Second edition 2021
The word list and the song lyrics may be photocopied by the purchasing institution or individual for class or home use. The story may not be photocopied or reproduced digitally without the prior written agreement of the author.